revival

revival

lindsay stribling

xulon press

Xulon Press
2301 Lucien Way #415
Maitland, FL 32751
407.339.4217
www.xulonpress.com

Paperback ISBN-13: 978-1-66286-996-9
Ebook ISBN-13: 978-1-66286-997-6

dedication

my story comes from you.
you should not be thanked for that,
and i write for you,
but more importantly for me–
for an understanding.
i may be the writer, but you will always
be the words.

trigger warning

i wrote this for my readers,
but my experiences may not agree.
this collection shares stories of
Emotional, Verbal, and Sexual Abuse,
Love, Heartbreak,
Suicidal Ideation, Self Harm,
Impulsive Actions, Drug Use –
be safe and be cautious.

table of contents

(intro)

the story of a girl so desperate to
find a way out, until she found it within
herself, her loved ones and God. you
too can have your own revival after love,
heartbreak, a tour of depression, and
much more, this is how i found mine.

we have a lot in common.
we are stuck in this world
with no exit from fear, emotion, or rage.
we're lost;
there is no ~~safe~~ escape.
here is my story,
my way out,
my rise upward.
here is...

my revival

the falling

i had been lying to myself
before you did
i called what you did love
in all honesty, there are too many
definitions of love
mine was you when it should
have been me.

a woman has had everything she
ever needed
until a man's words convinced her
she did not
i don't believe in the cliche, 'you love her
one day and the next you don't'
it isn't possible to decide how you feel
and come to such a quick resolution
you love her,
you love her not.
no.
i believe we fall out of love the same way
we fall in.
another cliche: 'slowly and then
all at once'
but no.
you love me,
you love me not.

everything was beautiful yet so
destructive
his smile so daybrightening yet so
fabricated
his eyes so deep and so elusive
his words so perfect yet so deceiving
his actions so right but so illicit
the way we fell in,
the way we fell out
and him
so beautiful yet so destructive.

maybe you did say it
and maybe i heard it
but i sure did not feel it.

you don't love me
i can feel that.

prices paid when i fell

the beginning of everything
falling apart
was when i began to fall for you.

day after day,
hour by hour,
you're there.
standing right there so happily,
and i watch you until you look at me.
you smile like you did when we first met,
or like the first day we fell in love.
we watch each other walk by
and abruptly every moment we ever
spent together flashed before us. every
kind word we spoke, every kiss we
shared, every laugh that almost had us
crying and everytime we cried together.
all the ways you would hold me in your
arms, and how you let me play with
your hair.
all the late night shenanigans and every
one of our favorite songs. every memory,
every hello and every goodbye... all there.
between us something was still there
but you kept walking
and so did i.

you used to love how i wrote
you never failed to remind me i had
such a gift and that my words were so
important.
my words, positive and negative,
were about you
i wonder if you ever realized,

i wanted you to love me the way you
loved my poetry.

i cannot tell if we are falling in or out of love.

i used to write your name on my arm
with glue. it would harden on my skin
and then i would peel it off letter by
letter. slowly.
it reminded me of our last days together.
agonizingly indifferent from the rest
until we reached the last letter and i
couldn't wait to rip you off.
but knowing i couldn't let you go on my
my own, i left it there waiting until you
fell off on your own.

this time i was not going to blame myself.

do not ask why
nor how or even when

i have no answer for the reasons why i
want you still.
i still feel your illicit hands moving all
over me each night. it keeps me awake. i
feel you crawling into my brain waiting
for me to cave so you can take me again.
i just want to sleep. so why am i thinking
about getting you back for one more
night. i still feel in danger around you but
that's why i liked you so much.
you loved to hurt me and i simply
loved the rush.

you never cared about my feelings,
but you promised me forever.
that was something i could hold onto,
even if i knew you would let go first.

i never gave you my emotions
not what i had in my heart
or maybe you couldn't receive it.
i was open to you
and you took what you wanted from me.
my entire body was yours,
the outside and even more
tragically, the in.
i gave you whatever you asked for,
including things that should not have
been for you
but i was for you
the way i felt for you had blown my
sail to sea
nowhere near you
nobody to you
if this is all i have left and if i am
going to die,
tell that selfish boy that i loved
him anyway.

this kind of paradise is not for
you, and you will start missing what
led you here.

        your dreams are chasing you
        now. by that i mean i am
            chasing you.

     we have been in a race for
years. neither you or i can
catch up with one another.

maybe we will have one
good day and then my
paradise will bore you.

each of my scars scream your name unknowingly that you are the reason they are there because loving you was the most self-destructive affair i have ever faced.

my own body became my home
the one thing i could depend on to never
do me wrong
the source of my confidence
my self-worth
and how i showed myself gratitude.
i tried to find a home in you
but instead you took mine away from me
and i had no place to go
so i let them come to me,
invading my home without knowing
it wasn't mine anymore
but yours in the way that
i am stranded waiting for my
strength back,
that so effortlessly lies in the palms of
your hands.
as did i
at your beck and call

like i said i had no place to go
no home of my own to return to
and no strength to be homeless.

in a way we both put our attention
toward my body.
you hurt it,
and i learned from you.

you came into my life pleading for
reassurance that you were normal.
begging for forgiveness like i was some
holy figure.
"i cannot fix you because you are not
broken," i say.
and you left, burning everything to the
ground on your way out.

your scent still lingers in my
bedroom sheets,
long after you left.
it reminds me of the days we spent
together and the nights we could
not sleep.
the serenity tries to wrap me in and band
me to you,
with
the scent of regret,
the scent of no mercy,
the scent of hatred,
the scent of you.

there is nothing stronger than
first love
other than the pain of first heartbreak.

she looks for the love she writes about.

i wanted so bad for you to be the one
who would
set my caged soul free. in my eyes you
were the one. the one sunflower in a
field of daisies. all my love had knotted
up waiting to untie into something much
more than incredible, with you. you
were the song i had playing on repeat
without knowing the title. but you, you
had your eye on her. the girl who knew
of infatuation but was near enemies
with the meaning of real love. that is
what i lacked. an innocence to the word,
thought and the idea of having something
pure. an innocence to pain. she was
merely a daisy in that field,
but she was your sunflower.

i was an accessory to you.
i couldn't convince myself that you
needed me to complete you.
just like your favorite sunglasses on a
sunny day.
to you, i was the bracelet you wore until
it was so worn down that it fell off due to
poor upkeep. insignificant.
i mean it was to you, you had no idea it or
i were gone.

i applied to work at the corner store
just across the street from where you live.
i transferred to your school.
i would ask your friends often how you
were doing, hoping you were breaking
without me.
but you were not without me.
i passed by your house everyday hoping
i could catch a glimpse of you, and each
time i saw you.
whether you were leaving or returning
home, even playing outside with your
younger brother.
until one day, i realized i hadn't seen you
in weeks and i crumbled.
i didn't know what you were
going through.
i couldn't see your smile or your
bright eyes.

all i knew was i couldn't be
there for you.
it was i who was without you and my
mind races to try to find an explanation
but it stops because you did not need me.
as for you, i was addicted and the
withdrawls became recognizable when
in every pair of eyes i saw you and who i
thought you were.

why did i let you kiss me on that
first day?

march 16th

it's not that i saw our end coming
but i knew i wouldn't be enough for you
i won't be mad at you for continuing
this routine
because i am not changing either
i sex away the pain
with people who mean but nothing to me.
this is my way of begging for your
attention.
and yours only.

just tell me i'm beautiful one last time
so we can stop putting each other
through hell.

i try so hard to figure out what it is
about you that makes me scream
i know
when i hear your voice, i get those evil
butterflies in my stomach, i run far, and
let my legs scream for me as i go.
i see your new girl and my knowledge
screams for her as a warning.
you kiss her, my eyes scream.
next thing i know you're coming my way
and my emotions scream praying upon
you for that acknowledgement that i have
not nor would i ever receive.
i watch you get in your truck where we
made so many memories and see you
drive away as my whole body screams for
your attention, we both knew you weren't
coming back.

i'm on my way home and my limbs
scream as they try to take me in your
direction, but i resist.
i get home and cuddle up in the
sweatshirt you gave me as my heart
screams at me wanting your body on
mine when our lips connect.

i scream for you, all of you, and only you.

i would be lying if i told you my mind
didn't travel back to that one night.
i don't know what made it so special.
maybe we were two lost souls who finally
found a home.
and i am homesick for you.

i had a dream that i saw you, i couldn't remember how long it had been.
you were sitting on the step below me and i moved to you soundlessly.
i don't know where we were but it didn't matter because we were there together.
you recognize my soft posture and elegant presence.
you turned to look at me with love and lust in your eyes, quizzical about which side would take over.
you then presented me with the sweetest hello and when you saw the slightest tear in my eye from disbelief, you let me fall right in your arms as if i hadn't ever left them.
it was you and i together again.
you couldn't take your hands off me and as in this dream,

i am latched onto you. i am afraid i will
keep telling myself the same thing but
never come face to face with you again.
it's sickening how much my eyes
missed you.

so please don't ever let me wake up.

you were all i ever wrote about
it was never about the love we shared or
our countless memories,
but the truth.
it was how you abused my sense of self
but now i'm going to beg for you to break
my heart one more time so i can get rid
of the writer's block.

if there was one thing or word i wish
u never said to me, it would be perfect. i
wish you didn't call me perfect.
if i was perfect then why didn't you fight
for me. how could you ever let me go
if that were true? if i was perfect you
would've showed me. even by a simple
thank you every once in a while. if i
was perfect, why didn't we last? if i was
perfect, why didn't you love me enough?
if i was perfect, then who's she?
is she perfect too? does her head fit right
under your shoulder like mine did?
are her hands small like mine?
does she rub her hands through your hair
the way you like?
do you laugh like we used to?
do you fight like we used to?

i'm on somebody else but
all i can think about is you and
everything we were.
how we were.
how we loved to touch and how we made
every moment our own,
who we were.
two romantics with an undeniable
connection. two teenage kids way in over
their heads for each other.
where we were.
lost but home within one another, our
love was everywhere we were.
what we were,
a beautiful pair made to meet.
and how i would die to have that again.

i said "it's okay".
i said it's okay because i wanted
to be okay.
i wanted to convince myself that you
did not hurt me because none of this
has hurt you.
i say it's okay everytime like it's a pattern
i'm locked in to following. you apologize
and suddenly we're doing what we do
best and it's okay to you.

you lost me way before you spoke
the words
"can we talk, i can't lose you"
but it was the words
"i just don't know how to fix this anymore"
that broke me in the end.

i pick apart every inch of myself
when you look at me.
is it my grown out roots?
tangled eyelashes?
that's the first thing i noticed
this morning;
or maybe my unplucked eyebrows,
or my crooked bottom teeth?
i should take better care of myself.
my grown out nails,
the acne on my cheeks?
it hurts too much to recognize i'm
failing me.
my famished jewelry and
tattered clothing?
the ones i've been living in for days.
my lopsided eyes and uneven freckles?
they never go unnoticed.

my right hand being slightly smaller
than my left?
the marks that obliterate my otherwise
stunning skin.
the hair on my arms.
the bumps on my thighs.
all the things i'd hoped you would
never notice.
i know you did.
you look me straight into my eyes and
tell me i'm perfect anyway,
perfectly imperfect for you.

you take advantage of the way i wish
to be loved by you
and combine it with the guilt i store
in my heart.
the guilt that screams at me when i speak
my truth and terrifies me into believing
this is what i want.
the guilt that tells me i must do it all for
you if i care to be good enough.
i know i am not it for you.
i wanted you to recognize how much i
had to offer without taking it all at once.
i wanted to give you my heart.
i wanted to place it ever so softly in
your hands,
to handle with care.
i wanted to give you my body,
for you to treasure.
i wanted to give you peace of mind,

a safe place for you to call home.
i wanted to give you all of my affection,
all of my compassion,
all of my love,
all of my words,
all of my thoughts,
all of me.
but before i could even reach my hands
out, yours were all over me.
grazing every inch of what wasn't yours
to take but mine to give.
pushing on every bruise, reopening
every scar,
scanning the sacred parts of me
and all i can do is pray you love me
when it's over

i wish i could stop thinking about all the things you did to me but there was nothing you did *for* me. you made me believe i was helping me when really it was all for you.

let me let go.

and in this case
you were you
and i was finally myself
your skin was my attractor
but your soul was my downfall.

i fell

i had been warned too many times about you and your intentions.

-i didn't listen

everything i do is for you but your
eyes are still on her.
i think i will finally admit,

i am jealous of the way she is
loved by you.

i could easily make a list
of all those i had lost,
but if any name should be first,
it's my own.

you see the picture while i'm stuck in
the mirror
they say the camera adds 10 pounds
but i want to erase 20
until i have nothing left for you to take,
for me to hate,
for you to destroy.
but the skin and bones that come with
the life i dread to live
if i am not smaller than this.

i was too busy convincing myself i was okay to ask for help.

there are parts of me that miss who i
was because despite all of the pain,
i had a way out
and i didn't do it for the pain
but because there wasn't any there
was nothing.
i was empty but i knew how to
fill the void.
i knew one thing; i was free.
i could do anything.
in contempt of my position i
jeopardize myself,
because i am broken.
i have no fix.
i feel like a part of me is scared to
heal because
i am not,
 nor will i ever be,
 good enough.

if i stay in misery,
i have an excuse for why i am
not complete,
nothing is right.
i start to feel good and then i can't take
it; i think i'd rather hurt myself than let
anyone else do it.
nothing is my own anymore.
my way of life has become
accustomed to yours
and everything was for you,
my mouth started mumbling words i
learned from you
and my hands began reaching to touch
things that did not belong to me,
like you,
touching me.
i caved for you
because my heart was enslaved to you,
so my body must be too.

my heart was trapped with you even
when i was trapped underneath you.

the funeral of us

we were almost silent.
i believe there wasn't a story where we
survived with our truth spoken voices.

so many instances close to death,
strung me along,
held me with a tighter grasp.

never yet had we hit rock bottom
where the devil was waiting to devour us;
all our evil in his hands.

but we were braver than his demise;
we stayed quiet,
hidden,
alone.

and we did not break until someone else
did it for us.

on my last legs i've failed again.
i broke,
i neglected,
i rebelled,
i hurt,
i lost,
and i left.
in all simplicity, the insanity loved to
mess with me

i wish i could make sense of the way
you treated me.
however, it's because i can't that i won't
ever be the same.

you stole my sensibility

i am the deaf. nothing of what you have
been saying is in my memory. i do not
recall a time where you have made
complete sense. i see you speaking but i
do not understand a word.

i am the dumb. no words can escape
from my mouth. you have tied me
down and shut me up. just as you
had hoped. you are here but the only
form of communication we can share
is nonverbal. nothing is more of a
punishment.

i am the blind. you have abused my
direction, where am i going? i am stuck
with no path to follow. you won't help me.
i am aware of your presence but you act
as if i am a nonentity.

i have nothing else for you.

you walk past me
and you ignore me.
you avoid looking at me,
anything that makes it seem like we
never met.
it's like you don't know me,
nothing about me,
but you never really knew me,
anything about me.
we were strangers then and now
how truly sick are you to be able to find
pleasure in my weakness.
it makes you happy to think that i cannot
get over you, and it brings you peace
when i cry,
but the only tear i ever shed for you
has a name.
she calls herself *regret*.

you said you missed me and in that
moment you were all i needed.
even if it was a dream, the feeling could
not be made up.
i wish it was your heart that said it and
not a fantasy in my mind.

a battle in your favor

today i've hit my breaking point
you had me locked in whether or not
you agreed.
your friends knew your story and mine
knew of the truth i shared,
but no one would figure us out.

i'm supposed to be fighting for
what's right,
instead, i'm fighting for you.
you promise you changed.
with you it's never different, i should
have known.

i tried to tell myself you felt guilty
for touching my body so wrongfully,
but i couldn't convince myself that was
the truth.
i'm lying to myself to protect you.

i need your love
or whatever it is you gave
me those months ago,

but since you are gone,
i guess it's fair to say
i won the, "i love you more," game.

i never realized what you did
until we were stuck in the middle of
our own mess.
it was your words and your actions that
made you the oppressor.
you were never for me.
i wish i had known how to fight.

break me down

i feel like i have been bored so i have
been out the door with what is right.
i am one foot in waiting for a love to pull
me in and consume me
so fast that i cannot breathe;
i want the excitement and the rush,
i want us.
but i am one foot out
remembering;

i have put up a wall.

you offered me the world
and i took it in my hands.
not knowing it was temporary.
that it would turn to dust and fall
through my fingertips, as i watched you
walk out on me.

when i think about what she
means to you,
i can't help but tremble
knowing i could not and will not amount.
i share my life with you.
but you keep half of yours hidden.
the love you have for her is so deep that i
cannot reach the broken parts of you.
i still try in ways to dedicate myself,
my well-being,
and my own health
to heal the wounds that burden you.
every broken part of me aims for every
broken part of you but every broken part
of you is still searching for her.

you didn't need that tattoo to
reassure yourself i'd be with you
when you go.

right when i met you, i knew just how our story would end.

only it was worse.

it was worse because i never thought i would love you as much as i did, and that's what made losing you so much harder.

i never wanted to admit that i was
your puppet, but i've been playing along
to your games as if you were my master.
i tried loving you,
that was a game too.

i keep having dreams about us and it
strengthens the hope inside me that
our spark isn't actually gone.
the way we see each other,
how you handled me with care,
and the way we speak;
it all felt so good and so real.
until i wake up
and i'm still the girl
that you won't ever love again.
but it's my fantasies that won't allow me
to let go.
i'll see you and us again tonight.

it was you who loved the way i looked
   next to you
it was you who cherished the fact
   that i couldn't wink no matter how
   hard i tried
it was you who admired how ticklish i am
it was you who fell in love with my eyes
   and the freckles on my cheeks
it was you who loved the way my
   knees twitched
it was you i cared for
it was you i wanted
it was you i would've died for
but it was you who broke my heart.

i'm mentally hooked onto the feeling
of being myself,
but i'm not quite latched.
because if i choose me,
then i lose you.
i can't decide if that is selfish.

what we had was suicidal
i couldn't save it, nor you.
no matter how hard i tried
that death had a hold on me.
my heart bleeds for you.
i'll have another bottle,
another pill, until i find that feeling again.

<u>water and a pencil</u>

to you, love was only a word
like water or pencil.
i tried so hard to make it mean
something to you,
anything at all.
whether it were the beautiful sunsets
over the mountains,
or the daisy in my hair;
it was for us.
but mostly for me.
and if that is selfish,
then it must be selfish for you to
expect me to care for you when you
disrespect me.
i am more than my clothes.
i am more than my body.
i am more than just a female.

it's selfish for you to justify me like that.
it's selfish that you let me love you.
i am nothing but a noun to you,
the water in my body,
the pencil in my hand.

i won't pretend to be hurt by your routine. i saw the end coming. i was just seeing how long it would take for you to get bored of me.

i waited years to find you and months
to finally talk to you. it took weeks to
build a friendship and only days after
that for me to realize how bad i wanted
you. one kiss to have me begging for
more, and only about two minutes for
you to break my heart.
hours for me to hate you.
a day for me to forgive you and one
week to want you back. but it will take
no less than an eternity for me to wish i
knew nothing of you other than your soft
brown hair and sweet brown eyes.
so for now, i will wait until you
want me again.

i fell in love with my body.
writing.
words,
yours and mine
hurtful and manipulative, truthful
and strong.
i fell in love with touch
from you or others.
i fell in love with
deceit:
the words that fell off our tongues.
i fell in love with demanding friendships
and codependency.
i fell in love with a lie that we
would be okay
and now i'm heartbroken because
we're not.

the words that screamed for me
are silent whispers,
and we are ghosts.
i am too young to not feel pain anymore.

falsified love

since day one i had convinced myself
you were good for me,
and that this was right. but deep down i
knew everything about us together was
wrong in almost every way. but neither
that, nor did anything else stop me from
falling back into your arms.

for years i had been asking for the
wrong things to strengthen me,

one: therapy. "we want to hear your
words, your feelings, your story," they
all say. once they know it all they send
you home with about four coping skills
and hopefully a smile even if it's fake.
theyattempt to fix you,
i don't need to be fixed...

two: promises. they lie to you.
"everything is okay," "you are ready," or
maybe even, "i love you." i relied on your
words and pushed away the deceit. but
you loved me, right?
i need proof not lies.

three: sunlight. nothing defines a person
more than the day and night. whether
she relies on the moon or sun for your
attention, the connection appeared. i had

defined myself as the solar eclipse, she
the moon tries to fall in line but can't ever
get there with her one chance,
but i do not need a definition.

four: time. they all told me how time is a
prescription. i had waited so long that it
was boundlessly outdated and i had the
wrong dosage. i gave all my time to him,
my time is precious, do not waste it.

five: drugs. actual drugs. i let my use
consume me and i cannot justify such
actions. i stopped thinking, learning,
moving. i stopped worrying. this is where
i fell. it won't let go.

i will not hold on.

and lastly, there was you.

i wish i had the courage to write a list
of all the people who have hurt me,
your name being first.
but it hurts too much to write,
nor you or i would be able to take that on.

he chose me, when you chose my body.
he liked my smile, you liked mouth shut.
he wiped my tears, you caused them.
we played board games and you played
mind games.
he came to the door, you waited outside.
it was sweats and a ponytail vs. tight
clothes and straight hair.
it was me vs. your expectations.
it was love vs. attention.
i thought i could get to you while i kept
him in my back-pocket.
i hurt him because you were
torturing me.
i broke him when you broke me.

on that first day a year later,
your memory hit me like the waves
crashing on the shore.
i could've been sucked right back in.
i won't forget the first day i saw you.
and i say that a lot but that day was the
start of our unexpected story,
the platform that shaped me for the rest
of my life.
i broke my rules for you
and i was living, not just surviving.
until they said your name,
and it wasn't your ocean that i had fallen
into but anyone else's,
anyone who would take me for the so
little i had left to offer.
i look for something good and sufficient
but i'm actually looking for the
impossible in you.

it's not that i want you back
but i almost die everytime your tide
rushes back out without me trapped
in between your sweet words and
convincing lies.
the distance has given me reason to love
you harder.
it's unbelievable how deeply i thought
about us making it to the end.

i will keep listening until our song is no longer beautiful.

for a great uncle of mine,

the thing that makes death so beautiful is
what we don't or can't understand.
what is it that turned off or shut down?
questions fill our minds.
it's a deception of life when we see who
or what it is that died lying at our feet.
the mystery of our next step is filled with
fear but also discovery.
it seems so close but it has never
been farther.
we all hear about how life is short
although its the longest thing we will
ever experience.
however it pains me effortlessly how
people die.
you were an angel on earth, and you still
live in my heart.

dear you,
this is not for another boy that
broke my heart.
this is for the somebody who affected
me the most.
you granted the biggest impact and the
hardest downfall.
i couldn't hate you.
you were supposed to be the one who
never left.
we were supposed to do
everything together.
i thought i would know you until the end.
you were the one who knew all the bad
stories but only shared the good ones
like i was perfect. but the only perfect
thing was that we never fell alone. we
were imperfect together.

how am i supposed to stand now? what
happens to all our foolish memories
and traditions? how am i to forget all
the countless times you were there for
me? why can't you put me back together
this time? am i supposed to pretend i
don't know you?
you were the one i could run to.
you were the one with a loss of judgment.
we were supposed to get through
everything like we shared the same
blood. i picked you up from every ditch.
neither of us were perfect so we were
imperfect together.
always and forever
no longer.
so to you,

i will never forget the way we used
to laugh. nor will i forget how strong
you made me.

    xoxo,
        your always & forever no longer.

i know i have no reason to be
apologizing, but i have a few last words
to say to you.
i'll start with,
i'm sorry i was not it for you,
i know i was good enough.
i'm sorry you couldn't see how badly i
wanted to love you,
i know i was worthy.
i'm sorry i fell so fast, i know where i
stand now.
i'm sorry that i still talk about you.
i'm sorry that i boast about my moving on
when you are all that is on my mind.
i know you think nothing of me.
i'm sorry that i keep waiting for you to
text me a simple, "how are you doing?"
knowing exactly what you meant:

"how are you without me? because i miss
you like crazy."
i'm sorry i have expectations for you even
though you left those months ago.
it's not my fault.
i wish i knew why i feel sorry. i wish i
knew why you left.

my good days

i refuse to say our memories are
indescribable.
it is our feelings that run wide.
it is not the words nor your touch, but
how we felt in those moments. those are
the moments i cherish.
i have become envious of who i was, ever
since i have been deprived of you.

it was the joy and dependency we felt
when we would laugh or speak. the
trust we built together. the love in every
action. the days our feelings couldn't be
relayed in any other words or actions.
i am not ready to let our moments
shatter, i am not ready to leave.

you are my good days and you are
indescribable.

intermission

halfway through writing this book
i began to contemplate once again
if i should change my theme. i felt it
came across as if i were suggesting
dependency on love and acceptance
from others..
no; i wrote it because i *felt* it – my
feelings are true. we all have a right to
our own feelings, no matter if they are
unfair or if people disagree or dislike
them. i wrote it because wherever i am
at in time, during this season, i was in a
demanding relationship with attention.
i will not disregard that. this is still my
revival and here is...

the rising

every year i take myself back to the
same place you stole everything from me
and i can't help but wonder if you
remember this day as well as i do.
i remember you feeding me with alcohol,
your very own poison.
i remember your hands tracing every
inch of my body
all over me
holding me down.
i remember your voice begging me
to give in
and your words
"you want this"
"trust me"
"be quiet"
i remember the look in your eyes
when i couldn't get out.
you had me.

i remember the locked doors
and the music you had playing.
i remember feeling choked but your
hands were elsewhere
and i was gasping for air,
pleading for your mercy.
i was so young and didn't know what it
meant to be strong
until you made yourself the victim and i
the oppressor
and i was forced to heal by my lonesome.

it's a tragedy what happened, what
you did to me.
and yet i feel sorry for you;
sorry that you couldn't respect me.
i told small-minded people who i thought
you could be and they looked at me so
foolishly.
i believed in you endlessly and you let me
down, time and time again.
you keep doing it because one, two, three
disappointments were not enough.
i thought i was the one pleading for my
innocence in your eyes but in fact you
were the one on your knees. how could i
have been so blinded into not seeing how
much more you needed me than i, you.
you hid your desires so well by
hurting me.

<u>may 16</u>

i thought that if i said yes tonight, we
would be considered equals in whatever
kind of relationship this is we have going.
you begged for me, but left once you got
what you were actually asking for.
proof again that your words should mean
nothing to me even if they sound so pure.

the dark part of me wants to see your
heart bleed.
i want to watch her leave stab wounds
in your skin and scratches on your soul.
i'd like to see her break you like you
did to me.
next time i say i'm here for you,
it's because i want you to fall
and i do not feel bad about that.

i tell them how you damaged me,
but never how harmful i could have
been to you.
i told them i loved you and that you did
not care about me or us.
that what we had meant nothing to you.
i still don't know if i believe any of
that is true.
i never opened up to you
but i was angry when you did the same.
neither of us took one another's pasts
into consideration.
we couldn't accept the struggle and i
never should have expected you to do
the things i couldn't,
we punished our hearts with compassion
while we were scared of the truth.

i thought he was it.
he was the one who was going to sweep
me off my feet and love me forever.
my delicacy rested in his hands.
we started so strong but ended so weak.
there was no more time for us.
he was the boy i dreamed about,
but that dream ended.
and with its end
came ours.

i won't ask how you have been most likely because i am scared that you are doing just fine without me. but there's also a piece of me that believes it's because you're not, and if i knew that, i would not be able to walk away.

i'm learning to say goodbye to someone who isn't actually gone.

i thought i could fix you.
i let my ego get in the way when all you
needed was love.
i left you at your lowest,
but only because i was lower
and every battle knocked me
down further.
i waited to see you grow
and you took my strength from me.
i waited for you and destroyed myself
while doing so.
i wanted you so bad i forgot what it
is i need.

a link to my childhood

i am in an endless turmoil; what feels
like a game of chutes and ladders.
i climb my way to a point but then i fall,
slowly slipping away from my best.
i remain constant but then lose my
confidence.
it's when i can't stay alright, when i
cannot climb anymore and when i fall
again and again and again,
i find i am stuck in a loop leading me
back to where i was when i met you. i
climb and then i remember the way
our eyes laid softly in one another's
emotional embrace,
i slide back to the day our eyes first said
hello as if my whole life had led up to that

moment when beautiful clouds and soft
ocean waves collide.
this game i keep playing is so dangerous,
but not like the way words flew from
your lips like a baby bird leaving the nest
for the first time.
you had a secret softside, and once i
found it you pushed me back down.
my blistered body and wounded soul
searched for nothing but your approval,
and i will stop at nothing until i
feel complete.
my final step is up ahead, the place
where i walk through your mind games,
past your words, avoiding your eyes.
i am stronger than you think i am.
i have manipulated your little procedure,
i am at the top and you are at the bottom,
begging for my mercy.

i want to find the ocean floor
although i have already hit the bottom.
and i am within myself.
all my attackers surround me with their
sharp teeth that tear deep inside my skin.
you are beneath me
but i have not drowned.

we associate depth with power
and you had your hold on me,
but i find my power when i rise.

i promise you by the time i'm over you
and you have left my mind
some part of you will be asking for me.
no one can erase your silent prayers.
i'm not thinking of you
and i am not in love with you.
but you,
you just realized i'm easier to leave than
to forget.
i'll crowd your mind until its unbearable.
you left me
but you never let me go.

this will be the day i can finally
say to myself
"you are good enough for you."

i think of myself before i ever
think of you.

and this time it's for you.
and now i possess you
for the next one that grows to love you
will be a part of my pity party;
she'll be laying in your bed by the time
she scrambles to put you back together.
i do not have you, but you have me. i'm
still there in the pieces on the floor that
fell from your broken heart.
she'll have to keep saving you when you
fall and it will take over her mind.
she's brainwashed, but you know in your
head why she's still there.
her touch, attention and overpowering
words mimic everytime we fell
continuously, almost as if you were the
one falling into my compulsion.
my blue eyes on her face.
my blonde hair on her head.
my body on you.
        i hope she knows i'm all of
            what's left of you.

i had stolen my power back from
you when i learned to love myself. i was
giving myself what i deserve.
i was strong enough until another of your
kind broke my heart.
for some reason i hated you for it, it was
like i disregarded what he did, but you
were the reason i was hurt in the first
place. it was your fault. i've been begging
for your attention for so long that it feels
normal to blame you. anything i try gets
dismissed so i taught myself to hate you.
you did everything right.

i am still a princess i'm just no
longer yours.

i had another dream about you last
night. a different you. him. a compilation
of all the great things we did together.
it was the way you let me just fall into
your arms the first time we met. like that
dandelion drifting in the air until in lands
softly on the well handled grass. the way
the sunset looked dull in comparison to
your soul.
i saw you again on the first day you
ever kissed me and that is where the
dream began.

there is something about new love
that tears the others to shreds.

because of you i felt
i have nothing left to write about but i
don't think i have ever been so wrong.
every emotion, every feeling, and every
ounce of love i have for you just simply
cannot be put into words. so all i can
say is i love you and pray you know
just how much.

on the last day of love, you held me in
your arms,
and i with so much more love to give laid
peacefully.
reminiscing on the times of our once
undeniable connection.
our fearless love.

you told me you liked my shirt
and my eyes,
my smile.
the way my hair lightens every summer.
you liked how easily entertained i
was by you,
especially when you kissed me.
you liked the music i listened to
and how i marched to the beat of
my own drum.
you told me you liked my shirt,
so i never wore it again.

i lost everything i ever knew trying to help you.
i never needed perfect. i didn't expect a prince out of you. but i couldn't be the only one trying to mend what we had. it was beautiful until it wasn't and it broke me when i broke you.

i knew by the way you looked at me that
something had changed.
even though i have been the same all
these months,
it was you.
it was you who no longer loved me.
it was you that changed,
and i wish it was me because i could
resent that
but you, i could never hate you.

i have recognized that the people in my life have created a rainbow...

red; my beautiful sister. she so fiercely entices the world around her. she boldly represents who any girl wishes they could be. her piercing eyes and stunning vision. she has the mentality to give selflessly and care endlessly. a spitfire type of girl in the best way possible. she holds her anger so deeply and rarely lets it show, but every shade of beauty shows through to me.

orange; the boy i met in therapy. someone new and exciting. an experiment to be sought out and handled with care. both of our hearts so fragile. a warning sign, with soft lips and illicit hands. the fire in my soul screams "danger" but i can't keep myself from you. safety was no longer positive or negative. between my anger and light. you were my median, my escape.

yellow; the girl i once called my best friend. i don't know who you are to me. our friendship was beautiful and you were the best and worst thing that came into my life, as much as i wish i could deny it. you always will be a sister to me, despite the questioning, i could never associate you with hate. your subtleness is so constant. a personality so indescribable in a girl so unforgettable.

green; the girl better than i. a mystery. whatever she wears, wherever she goes and whoever she is. it's the way she walks or talks and the way her hair falls. she's simple but so complex. i envy the way

she lives, the attention she receives. i
can't ever be her. the way she opens
up, the way she parties. how she gets
to who i am in desperation of a simple
glance from her. her perfect figure and
breathtaking voice. the girl i wish was me.

blue; the first boy i fell for. his aqua-
gray eyes and the way they fell into
mine. his sudden sadness at any given
moment. he would come over for a kiss
and then leave. how he entered my life
so degradingly and then left so easily. he
was so willing to use me. the financial,
sexual and emotional abuse nearly killed
me. your supposed love consumed me.

purple; the beautiful, evil consistency
of people walking in and out of my life.
constant rage that turns into loneliness,
never apart but always alone, far from

who i should be. nothing makes sense other than begging for you back, but for myself, i will not do that. purple is my courage.

i look back and fail to recognize the girl in the pictures. the girl who spared everyone the truth that she was the girl infatuated with attention. the girl who needed to be a part of you and would do what you did just because you did it. the girl who hurt herself over and over hoping you would realize how torn she was between loving you and loving herself. the girl who needed your approval when you didn't need her consent. the girl who gave every part of who she was to you, to change. to shape into the girl you wanted because that is all she wanted to be.
this girl is not who she wanted to be.

there was so much more i could have said or would have done to keep you from leaving but i respected you too much to burden you with that.

it was finally my turn to get the love i
had given so well,
but that was stripped from me.
as much as i would like to say it wasn't
my fault,
it could not have been anyone else's.
you were perfect,
and the others were trying to protect
you from my words,
from the hatred in my heart,
the hurt and envy i bear.
i come with strings that you were
willing to play,
not as a game but with so much beauty.
the sound of our music was beautiful
until you were taken from me.

i remember the days i pleaded to love
you , and i remember the day it stopped.
you don't.
you were first and with you left a
part of me.
stolen in the glance of everything
we ever had.
i remember when we had it good.

since you said those words to me a
time ago, they have been on repeat in
my mind. perhaps i can't get enough
of your voice or is it that i'm hoping it
wasn't actually goodbye and you still
love me too?

as unfair as it is,
i'll blame you for the way others have
hurt me since you've been gone.
so the pain turns into anger
because that is something i can learn
to manage.
i won't ever stop loving the person you
showed me you can be
and i won't ever hate you in contempt of
the horrid ways you treated me.
and because i'll always care,
i will rack my brain
until i don't miss you anymore.

it was almost my excuse.

a friend of mine once told me she
knew she had been in love because she
was still so hurt.
she encouraged and convinced me i had
fallen too hard and it had become the
very reason i was so inconsolable,
i let myself believe i loved him.
i loved his smile
i loved his desire
and i loved his grace.
but that meant i had to love how
unreliable he had become
and had to love how he served me with
such disrespect.
but overall i had to love that he would
never love me.

i let myself believe i loved him.

you lean on me like a trap i could never
let myself fall into.
codepency.
how can you place that pressure
on another?
to not be able to make up your own mind,
to not have your freedom,
an escape.
freedom is writing and it does not
entrap me,
i can breathe.
i can release every thought, every feeling,
and every soul that keeps me from being
my own person.
i escape through my words, as does every
worry i may have.
to be codependent on another would
strip me of my free will.
i will not make that sacrifice.

belonging

i am not yours.
i was never yours.
and i won't ever be yours.
but there was one moment where you
held me so close,
everything fit–
my head on your chest,
your hand in mine.
i knew i wanted this to last forever
and then i remember,

i am not yours.
i was never yours.
and i won't ever be yours.
but because of those moments i
know a part of my heart will always
belong to you.

you're hiding in your kingdom
some place.
i can't see who you used to be,
my knight in shining armor ready to
make me queen. his queen.
i loved you.
once i found you, you were still lost.
i don't recognize you, and to you i
am nobody.
like i said, i loved you.
and i say that i loved you
because i wish that i could have.
in the lengths that
we *could* have shared something great,
we *would* have been great.
we *should* have been great.

at least i was good to you
and i hope you remember that about me.
i hope you remember how patient i
was with you,
i would've waited a lifetime.
i hope you remember my endless effort
to be enough for you,
and that you remember how careful i was
with your heart.
i hope you remember the way we lit up
around each other and how strong our
love truly was.
despite the fact i was not the girl for you,

i hope for the right girl
you would give all your love and all
your effort,
you would rise to your full potential and
be the man i never got to meet.
i hope for the right girl, you change.

dear me,

i'm sorry that i let you prioritize others above yourself. i'm sorry i allowed you to heal other people without giving you enough time to heal your own wounds. i'm sorry that you tried so desperately to please others when all you needed was my approval. i'm sorry you put all your attention toward what they wanted other than what you needed. i'm sorry i let him hurt you. i'm sorry that smiling hurt daily but i forced it out of you so no one had to worry about you. i'm sorry there were days you cried yourself to sleep and no one was there. i'm sorry i allowed you to fall down the wrong path. i'm sorry i let you believe you were not good enough. i'm sorry i lost who you once were. and i'm so sorry i did not love you in the way you deserved to be loved.

but i promise you, you are on your way
to revival
and i'm sorry i didn't lead you
there sooner.

i rose

i once wanted you
and now i don't.
it's not regret i feel
but remorse that i let myself fall
prey to you
and relief that i survived.

m.b.

i fish in the wrong sea
because after i lost you
i thought i would never find
someone so real,
so honest,
and so so good to me.
thank you for teaching me
i deserve better than before.
thank you for making me realize
i am capable.
thank you for teaching me to turn my
anger into art.

i remember the way you
looked that day.
the day i knew you would forever be
irreplaceable.
the sparkle in your sweet brown eyes
spoke to me in the way no words
ever could.
you watched me run from down the hall
as i leaped into your arms and you spun
me around like a princess.
you set me down and the only thing on
my mind was "i found him".
i found my prince charming and this was
my fairytale.
you ever so lightly pressed your lips on
mine, and with a grin from ear to ear,
you told me i taste like raspberry.
i was wearing raspberry lip gloss.

this was the moment i waited for
all my life.
the moment i felt as if i was meant
for more than the life of an average
teenage girl.
you were my dream and you shall be my
dream forever.

i fell in love with a boy far out
of my reach.
with nothing but words through the
phone, not a single touch.
i wonder how tall you look standing next
to me and if our hands fit as perfect as i
imagine they will.
i wonder if your mom is still as excited to
meet me as i am her.
i wonder if you know i wear my
necklace everyday.
i wonder if i can make you laugh the way
i did through facetime and watch your
eyes light up when i tell you i love you
more than anything.
because i do,
love you more than anything.

i'm still trying to figure out how it is
possible to love someone that lives 500
miles away,
someone that i've never even met.
but it just makes sense,
you make sense
we make sense.
the fact that i have gained all this love for
you without so much as a kiss, in some
way, makes sense.

as much as i would like to let
you back in,
i know you would never love me the way
i love you.
so instead, i will learn to forget you.

when i had to start begging for your attention,
i didn't want it anymore.

if i could get a second goodbye,
i would tell you how you changed me.
now i believe i can be more.
i am worth more than i lead on.
you were the one who spoke your words
and meant them;
you opened my eyes to so much more.
i would tell you how you inspired me to
be the beautiful writer i am
and to live life in the moment,
to be who we truly are and to
love ourselves and each other for
that honesty,
to accept and build on who i am.
you gave me gifts i can't ever return,
but this time it's not okay and i won't say
the words that mean you leave forever.
so until next time,
my mystery of love,
since this time wasn't right.

we were not meant for forever.
although i thought we would have lasted
longer than we did. maybe in my head we
did and that can explain why it's been a
year and i am still writing about you.

<u>kamilla Sandoval</u>

i developed an interest in art,
not just writing but painting as well. i
never realized how beautifully expressive
it could be in such a poetic way.
i combine my arts.
most of my writing would be painted over
with black
like it wasn't ever there
but this is now your color.
you put the light in my art.
the immediate beauty reflects and relates
to the art form.
you are my art
and it's only you
because baby your soul is golden.

i see countless people on the streets
begging for money, willing to do anything
for their fix- homeless, waiting for
a miracle.
i don't know if i feel jealousy or sadness.
but i feel for these people.
it is inconsiderate to tell someone in a
different situation that you understand.
i have a home
i have a family that supports me
and i am fortunate but i do understand
i see myself, in the mirror as broken,
willing to do anything for my fix, which
in this case is any sort of attention, and
god bless anyone who helped me, i was
homeless in my own body
but now my body is my miracle.

for the boy i consider to be my first
real love,
i know i am not it for you. i've known for
a while. and why i can't let go is because
you loved me despite everything i picked
apart about myself. to you i felt like the
perfect image of the woman you wanted
to be with. it breaks my heart to know i'm
going to hurt you but it's inevitable. to
me, you were never the boy i wanted to
marry and as much as i want you right
now i don't want you forever. i told you
i did and i lied to protect you but what
you needed was protection from me,
protection from pain. and as much as
i wish i could have given you that, i'm
going to hurt you. what i can do now is
be as selfless as i can with pure honesty.
even though you see it reversed, this is
for you because you deserve to thrive

and to find the girl who will motivate you
to be your best self. the one who wants
to be with you on your worst days. i wish
so bad and pray so hard you find the
girl who would die for you. you deserve
someone who is sure of who she is with
you, not i who held you as a crutch. not
i who used you to feel beautiful and
appreciated. not i who didn't deserve
your heart. you deserve someone who
won't hurt you.

not i who inevitably will break your heart.

for the short time we were together
my words went to you.
i had nothing to write.
what we had was perfect,
right from a fairytale,
but i am not a perfect writer
and this is much less than a fairytale.
i didn't love you
but i know i could've.
you closed my heart,
but opened my eyes
and i am writing again.

we had it so real.
every word so genuine,
and i don't hate you for leaving only
because you showed me the importance
of communication.
you showed me how honesty can spare a
heartbreak.
you leaving did not break me but it
opened me.
i may have ended meaning nothing to
you but i am okay with that because i
know there was a time when i was your
everything.
i go through our old messages
and remember how much fun we
used to have,
the hidden laughs and slight smiles,
all the plans we made and every time you
said good morning and good night.

i remember how much i cared about you,
never mind how much i still care.

you showed me such kindness and for
that i will finally let you go because you
deserve whatever it is that is going to
help you *rise*.

i would always worry i was never the
right amount of anything.
"i was never good enough for him"
and everything i did was wrong.
my intentions were of something so
indescribable in the most positive way.
of something so so good and pure, to
say simply.
and the both of us were well aware of
the lengths
i would go for your happiness.
but i was still insufficient, i knew it and
i'm sure he did too.
right now would probably be the
part where i would write about how
he shattered my heart, and there is
nothing wrong with that but we are
switching it up.

as i grew through these experiences,
so did my writing. almost as if we
matured together.
and there may be no repair to the
damage he bestowed upon us
but he did not break us.
we are growing,
we are strong,
and we do not need him,
for we are complete.

i thought you were good and good for me but you had routines that changed my mind, and now that it's over i'll never let you have me again.

thank you for breaking me

i used to hate you
and what you did to me,
how you changed who i was
and not necessarily in the good way.
and i had fallen,
i had been lost,
i had been stranded
far away from you–
my home,
my only friend,
and you were the only one to blame.
they all say i had every reason
to hate you
but that was far from my beliefs.
for everything you had done to change
me has shaped me into who i am today
and by hating that, it would be
impossible to love myself.

loving my body does not make me
unchristlike.
it makes me strong,
for having gone through what i did and
for continuing to treasure myself.
i love who i am and you have not
defeated me.

i am sorry you only knew the part of
me you saw in pictures because i am so
much more than my appearance.

i'm not used to being cared for
i'm not used to having so much fun with
someone so perfect for me.
it's nice to be kissed with no hands
running down my body.
it's refreshing to feel something other
than lust.

this is not love yet
but this is life.

and we were in love without a care in
the world.
sometimes we'd just drive
and we'd end up at the city's end...
or in the woods...
or a whole new town.
it could've been terrifying
but with him
everything was simple.
we were in love without a care in
the world.

i see the way you are with me, and nothing in my life has made greater sense.

i fell in love with the boy who never let
me touch a door
or pay for dinner.
i fell in love with the boy who could sit
and talk to my mom for hours at a time.
i fell in love with the boy who made me
feel like the only girl in the world.
i fell in love with the boy who engrained
his voice in my head,
my lips on his,
my body all over him.
i fell in love with the boy who cherished
every moment like it could be the last;
one last kiss before you go.
you are engraved in me:
mind, body, heart, and soul
all for you.
i fell in love with the boy

who payed attention to the detail
in my eyes
and could sink so deep into them.
i fell in love with boy who prioritized my
self worth,
the boy who would drop anything to
protect my heart at all costs,
the boy who created a safe space in his
arms so perfect there was only enough
room for me
no matter where we were.
i fell in love with the boy who treated me
the way i deserved to be treated,
the boy who treated me like a princess
when i didn't feel like one
and lifted me so high on that pedestal.
i could finally see clearly that this was
my destiny.

i am at a point in my life where i am
perfectly happy and i see the future
ahead of me clearly.
the house we talked about with so
much land.
a wrap around porch with a white picket
fence. everything i'd dreamed of and i
can't help but wonder if i dreamed too
small or if you truly are my destiny. if our
souls were meant to meet like you said.
i ask if there's more for me but all i see
is you. more of you. more laughs. more
memories. more effortless love. more you
is all i can dream for now and forever.

as much as i hate the word forever it feels so right saying it to you.

i want nothing that i had with
him for us.

and i want everything we have
now forever.

and i don't want that with anyone else.

and you, if i ever lose you, i want
you to have days that feel like magic.
kisses that take your breath away. make
memories that remind you of love songs.
i hope the stars reach your soul and lift
you up the way i tried so temperately
to do. i await the day you learn to love
who you are, the way i do. we both
know i loved everything you hated about
yourself.
i want you to take our memories and
start over. lose the ghost inside you and
find your home. even though i did see
you at your worst without a thought
of leaving you, i want you to be more. i
believe you can be you.
i will forever have a hold on you, like you
do on my heart.
and i won't let go until you are
strong again.

it's six in the morning and this is
the first time in months i had woken
up so early.
i wiggle my toes underneath the covers
and listen to the birds chirping.
how beautifully they sing, was my
first thought.
not how much i loved you,
not how much i miss you,
but the melody of recovery.
the melody of i am in love again.
not with you
but with the way the sun always rises
after it sets.
i am in love with chai lattes on the porch
with my favorite blanket and a new book.
a melody of revivals.
i am in love with new ideas and new days.

good morning to a new start.

openness is how to describe this near fantasy.

a wide field of color: the brightest pinks and softest yellows.

nothing i've seen has been more serene. the peace within me is everlasting, the peace that makes me long to stay here forever.

running through the hills reaching into the clear air, with the sun shining on my skin, and the wind brushing through my hair.

unknown is ahead of me and i can't help but venture.

i seek further peace although i don't know if that is possible, but in a place like this all is possible. i want to stay here forever.

i tried so hard to be the girl any other
girl wished they could be.
i tried so hard to get better all
    on my own.
i tried so hard to say no.
i tried so hard not to let him take
    advantage of me
i tried so hard not to let the addiction get
    the best of me.
i tried so hard not to fall in the
    wrong crowd.
i tried so hard to mean more than
    just my looks.
i tried so hard to be different than
    everyone else.
i tried so hard to be honest at therapy.
i tried so hard to be prettier and skinnier.
i tried so hard to be good enough for
    anyone or anything.

i tried so hard to be his, when all i really
   needed was to be mine.
i try for myself.
so finally this is for me, and only me.
and i'm sitting here smiling like an idiot
because it has never felt so good to care
for myself.

there's a special person in my life that
i think so highly of yet she can't find the
confidence in herself to believe what i do.
to remind you my soul sister,
your passion for everything you have is
unbelievable and can't be beat.
your immense sense of who you are as
a person has brought me to believe i am
who i was meant to be.
you instill it in me that i am worth
the world and i wish for you to
believe the same.
i knew if i only had you in this world i
would be okay but without you i wouldn't
be who i am.
and it's because you are my lifeline.
you are important.
your soul is so genuine and true.

your effort, willingness and
determination do not go unnoticed.
you truly are the most beautiful person i
have ever known,
like the heart you put all your weight on.
let that weight go and believe that
the love you store in your heart is
capable of loving yourself like i do.

what are you worth to yourself?
- i am more. more than what you have
to offer, not because you are not enough
but because i am worthy. worthy of
what's next. not the next fail but my
upbringing. i'll get lost but i'll find myself
again and again. you were not the end of
me. i have more. more life in me. more
to offer. through writing and words and
through knowledge. i am more in the
know about what happens to girls my
age. i won't be taken for granted again.
i am able to look past deceit and find
what is good for me. i can say no. i have
boundaries. i am healing. i am so much
more than my appearance. more than my
past. more than my story. more than the
lies. more than you will ever see me to
be. i can't be played for a fool and i won't

allow another man to tear me down. i don't have any tears left. i can finally gain weight. i can be good for myself. i don't have to want you anymore. i don't need your approval. i approve of everything i have set up for myself by myself. i did it for me. there is so much more for me. and i can thank myself because i am more. i am more after what you did to me. i am more because i survived. i am more because i am myself and that is everything i could ask for and more.

i cannot give up   i will fall down   i can

i will not give up   but i will get up   i will

i cannot give up   i will fall down   i can

i will not give up   but i will get up   i will

i cannot give up   i will fall down   i can

i will not give up   but i will get up   i will

i cannot give up   i will fall down   i can

i will not give up   but i will get up   i will

i cannot give up   i will fall down   i can

i will not give up   but i will get up   i will

i cannot give up   i will fall down   i can

i will not give up   but i will get up   i will

i cannot give up   i will fall down   i can

i will not give up   but i will get up.   i will.

the way you speak to yourself matters
you are beautiful and i love you
(thank you, dad)

i'm finally where i need to be in
life and have the most appreciation
for myself,
that i allowed myself to heal
and be who i am so worthy of being.
believing i am who i was meant to be
and loving every ounce of my
imperfections that make me myself.
my selfishness came from a place
of wanting so bad to heal but not
knowing how.
i give it all to myself for letting my pride
go and loving myself to my core.
the next stage isn't far ahead and i
pray to take this knowledge with me
for i know
that is not my last heartbreak
and that is not the last time i will
feel pain

or feel like nothing.
but this is the first time i have taught
myself healing
and what it takes to find that
inside myself.
this may not be the only revival in my
life but it sure was the one that taught
me to, no matter what, appreciate what
god gave me.
my body for one, i will show u care.
my heart, i will put you first.
my mind, i will consider you valid.
my all, you come first.

God allowed the people to trust him
by trusting they would follow his word.

through Elijah, God said he would
provide if they continued to fight and so
they did. he never let the oil run dry or
the flour to run out. he provided for the
ones who believed they were a lost cause.

he provided me with a purpose.
a purpose to write.
my way out.

God gave me My Revival.
thank you.

(acknowledgments 1)

for my best friend, my twin sister, my all in 1 for caring about me endlessly despite how many mistakes i have made. for picking me up off my knees everytime i fell. this is for never failing to inspire me. your beauty is rooted so deep and your light shines through so easily. your heart is stunning and your care is effortless. you are my greatest influence. this is for giving me my strength back. i look at you and see the best version of me. the bond we have is unlike any other sibling relationship and no amount of love will measure up to this. i guarantee us living this life together was no mistake. thank you for being my rock and for reminding me i already have my person for life.

(acknowledgements 2)

this is for my mom, nothing means more to me than the endless effort you put in for my happiness. what you do not realize is that you are my happiness. you are the reason i smile everyday. the reason i believe there is a way out and there is nothing nor anything i can give to you that will amount to the love you show for me and because of that our bond will last forever. you are half of me and i cannot thank you enough for making me who i am today. i will forever be grateful for the fact that you have never left my side and have become my best friend.

i love you always.

for my dad,
you were the one who reminded me that i am worthy of all love. this is for teaching me to speak kindly to myself. so for you,

i cannot give up, i will not give up. i will fall down, but i will get up. i can, i will.
thank you for loving me and showing me how to love myself. you are my strength.

for the Thompsons, Delforge and Stribling families,
you have all encouraged me to pursue my dream and have helped me on my journey. your constant efforts are the gift that i cannot ever thank you enough for.

for my sisters,
thank you for living this life with me. for growing and learning with me. thank you for always having my back. you are both beautiful and i'll love you forever.

for my first love,
my greatest treasure you were. you taught me what love was and for that there are no words

sufficient enough to thank you. there will always
be a piece of my heart that belongs to you P.

for Zachary,
you taught me to have the greatest appreciation
for life and showed me how worthy i am to live
here. i will never forget the feeling i first felt
with you, the feeling of true revival and that this
world was meant to hear my words.

for Natalie Minkler and Leah Lindholm,
for traveling with me through the epic roller
coaster we call life and never letting me fall
alone. you are my sisters and you are golden. i
pass this on to you, it's your turn to rise.

for all my teachers and supporters,
thank you for believing in me and guiding me
here. i would be nowhere without your support.
thank you for your understanding.

(acknowledgements 3)

for my lord and savior, thank you for instilling in me the power to be the writer i am. thank you for having my back and believing in me from day 1. i will eternally be in your debt.

and for you,
for reading my words and hearing my story. for making my dreams come true.

to be able to thank you all is a blessing.

About the Author

Lindsay Stribling grew up in Southern Arizona in the United States and has had a passion for writing ever since elementary school. She would write stories for others to enjoy until she realized the beauty of her writing lied in poetry. She began seriously writing in the beginning of her freshman year when her life took a turn. Little did she know writing was her way out, her words went to the pages before her fears could expose themselves. This first collection of hers is her story and how she survived. Now attending Northern Arizona University, she knows there is nothing she wants to do other than help others through her writing.

for the **National Sexual Assault Hotline Call 800-656-4673**. a member of the staff will be available 24 hours a day, 7 days a week.

if you are thinking about ending your life please use what i can give you, call <u>The National Suicide Prevention Hotline 800-273-8255</u>.

SAmHSA's National Helpline is here to help (in English and Spanish) for individuals and families facing mental and/or substance use disorders. call <u>1-800-662-HELP (4357)</u>.

there are people who care about your story and your recovery. your life is precious and deserves to be lived to the fullest. there are people who are going to help you with your revival. you will rise.

i am a 16 year old girl, and this is my story. i consider myself a social activist, especially a feminist. one of my many reasons for being a feminist is because of the things i've experienced myself, at such a young age. the earliest memory that i have of being harassed is from when i was in the second grade. i went to a school that had all grades in one building, so that meant i rode a bus with high schoolers. i was so young and i just wanted the older kids to think i was cool and mature, so i went and sat in the back of the bus with them. there was this one guy who looked to be about 17 years old who introduced himself to me and this other girl who was my age. he made small talk for a little but, until he decided to ask a very personal question, one that involved our private areas. i didn't know what it meant and why he wanted to know, but i answered anyway. i never told anyone because i didn't think it was an inappropriate question to ask a 6 year old. i don't remember much about what happened after. that was only the first incident i had that year. a few months later, i met a girl a few grades above me and we became friends. we would hang out at each other's' houses all the time. one day she kissed me on the mouth without asking me. i was taken back, but didn't really mind because i just thought she was being friendly. and then she decided to put her hands down my pants and touch me. i didn't like it, but i let her because i didn't want the older girl to hate me. since i let her do this, she kept

doing it everytime we would hang out.
it made me feel so uncomfortable and
upset all the time, but i wanted to be the
cool younger girl that had older friends.
i now realize, she was just using me.
these are just a couple situations that i
have been put in as a young girl. i shared
these because i feel as though they make
me who i am today. i am not ashamed,
nor do i feel like any if the things i've
experienced are my fault. i want to use
my voice to share with people who may
have shared similar experiences with
me that it's not their fault if scary things
like that happen to them. it will never be
your fault. i will always use my voice to
advocate for things like this.

- anonymous

send your stories of revival to:

lindsaystriblingpoetry@gmail.com